Abraham Lincoln

Christi E. Parker, M.A. Ed.

Table of Contents

Who Was Abraham Lincoln?

Abraham Lincoln was the president of the United States during hard times. The people of the United States argued about many problems. The most important issue was slavery.

Lincoln was against slavery. But, he wanted to keep the country together. He did not want the southern states to **secede** (suh-SEED) from the Union. These disagreements and others led to the Civil War.

Lincoln's Early Years

Abraham Lincoln was born in a log cabin in Kentucky. The Lincoln family did not like slavery. When Lincoln was seven, his family moved to Indiana. Slavery was not allowed there.

Lincoln only went to school for one year. He liked to read, and so he studied on his own. It was not until he was an adult that he finally had a teacher help him. Lincoln was very smart and learned things quickly.

▼ Southern slave auction

An Image That Stayed with Him

Abraham Lincoln witnessed a **slave auction** (AUK-shuhn) as a young child. He saw slaves kept in pens waiting to be sold. That horrible image stayed with him for the rest of his life.

In 1830, when Lincoln was 21, he moved to Illinois. There he had many jobs. He even studied law books and became a lawyer. Lincoln ran for a county political office but lost. He did not give up. Two years later, he won a seat in the Illinois government.

▼ An evening in the log cabin

Working His Way to Washington

In 1842, Lincoln married Mary Todd. Mary was from a rich family in Kentucky. She met Lincoln when she moved to Illinois. They had four sons. Sadly, three of the boys died when they were young.

Lincoln ran for a United States Senate seat in 1858. He ran against the current senator, Stephen Douglas. Douglas was a very powerful man.

Mary Chooses Lincoln

Mary Todd dated both Lincoln and Douglas. She fell in love with Lincoln and they were married. Sixteen years later, Douglas won the senate election, but Lincoln still had Mary's love.

Abraham Lincoln and his family

▲ Lincoln and Douglas debating in Illinois

As the two men traveled through Illinois, they held **debates**. These debates took place in train stations. Thousands of people came to watch the two great men speak. The men debated over slavery and states' rights.

Lincoln did not feel that the government should allow slavery. Douglas thought people should decide for themselves about slavery. Though Douglas won the senate election, Lincoln did not give up. Two years later, he started a new campaign.

Lincoln Is Elected President

In the year 1860, Lincoln ran for president of the United States. He was a member of the new Republican Party. His main competition was Stephen Douglas, again.

Lincoln did not believe in slavery. He said he would leave it alone in the states that allowed it. However, he did not want slavery to spread to the new states. Lincoln's main goal was to keep the Union together.

Where Was Lincoln's Name?

In the South, Lincoln's name was not even printed on some of the ballots. The Southerners thought Lincoln would force them to end slavery.

1860 campaign banner ▶

▲ Lincoln giving his inauguration speech

Lincoln won less than one-half of the **popular vote**. There were three other candidates, and no one won a **majority** of the votes. However, Lincoln received the most **electoral** (uh-LEK-tor-uhl) **votes**. So, he became the sixteenth president.

▲ The Civil War began at Fort Sumter in Charleston, South Carolina.

The War Begins

The Civil War officially began on April 12, 1861. This is when the first shots were fired. However, the war really started when states seceded from the Union. The first state to secede was South Carolina. Other states quickly followed.

In 1861, Lincoln ordered weapons to be made for the northern army. At the same time, he increased the size of the army and navy.

Lincoln still did not want to interfere with slavery. But, he did not think the country should split apart. Lincoln quoted the Bible when he said, "A house divided against itself cannot stand." He wanted to save the Union.

Accidental Deaths

There was no one killed during the actual bombing of the fort. However, two Union soldiers were killed and two more were wounded when a cannon exploded during the evacuation of the fort.

▼ Attack of Fort Sumter by Confederate troops

Lincoln Frees the Slaves

Once the war started, President Lincoln decided to free the slaves. In September 1862, Lincoln announced the **Emancipation Proclamation** (eh-man-suh-PAY-shuhn prah-kluh-MAY-shuhn). This document stated that the slaves in the southern states would be freed.

The **Border States** were slave states that shared borders with free states. During the Civil War, most of these states stayed with the Union. The Border States included Delaware, Maryland, Kentucky, and Missouri. Lincoln did not end slavery in these states. He was afraid the states would secede if he ended slavery there.

Slaves in the South were finally freed in 1863.

The Time Was Right

Lincoln did not want to free the slaves until after the North had a military victory. At the Battle of Antietam, the North and the South tied. But, this was the first time that the northern army looked good on the battlefield. Lincoln thought it was a good time to announce his proclamation. He hoped it would keep the North going and force the South into defeat.

▼ After the Battle of Antietam, President Lincoln visited the battlefield.

Honoring Those Who Died

The Battle of Gettysburg (GET-teez-buhrg) was the first major victory for the North. This battle happened July 1–3, 1863. The war had been going on for two years. Many historians think of this battle as the **turning point** in the war.

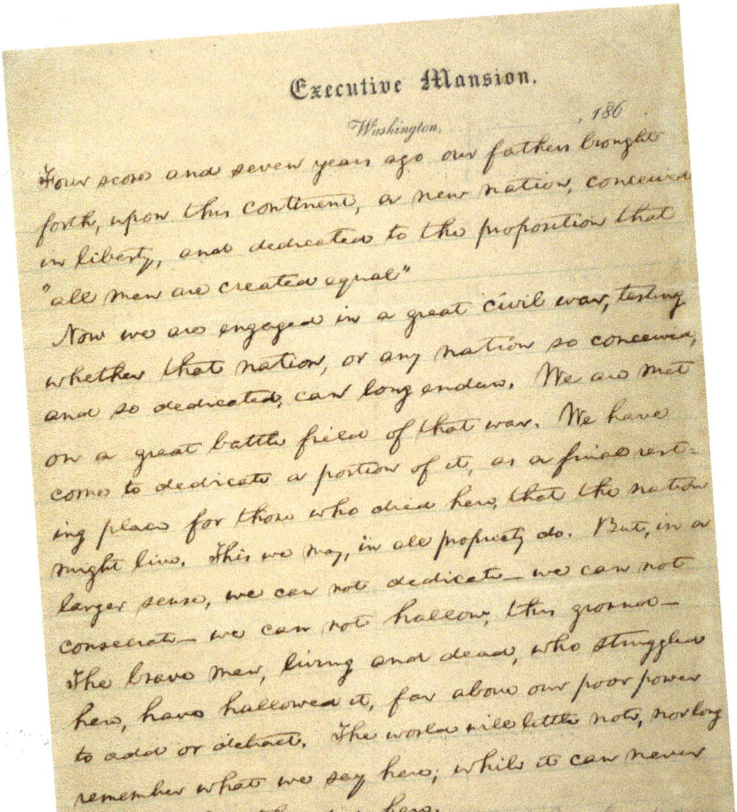

Executive Mansion,

Washington, , 186 .

Four score and seven years ago our fathers brought forth, upon this continent, a new nation, conceived in liberty, and dedicated to the proposition that "all men are created equal"

Now we are engaged in a great civil war, testing whether that nation, or any nation so conceived, and so dedicated, can long endure. We are met on a great battle field of that war. We have come to dedicate a portion of it, as a final resting place for those who died here, that the nation might live. This we may, in all propriety do. But, in a larger sense, we can not dedicate—we can not consecrate—we can not hallow, this ground— The brave men, living and dead, who struggled here, have hallowed it, far above our poor power to add or detract. The world will little note, nor long remember what we say here; while it can never forget what they did here.

It is rather for us, the living, ~~to stand here~~, we here be dedica

Not Long Remembered?

Lincoln did not think he did a good job with his speech. He called his Gettysburg Address a failure. It was not even reported by some newspapers. In the speech he said, "The world will little note, nor long remember what we say here . . . ." This is not true. Today, this speech is considered to be one of the greatest speeches in United States history.

▼ Gettysburg National Cemetery

One-third of the men who fought at Gettysburg died. A national cemetery was built at the battle site. It **honored** the men who died there.

On November 19, 1863, President Lincoln helped **dedicate** the cemetery. He gave a short speech to honor the soldiers. The speech was called the Gettysburg Address. It lasted just two minutes and was only 272 words long. But, his few words are still remembered today.

General Ulysses Grant took over command of the Union army in 1864.

Finding a General

For the first two and a half years of the war, Lincoln could not find a good general to lead his army. He changed generals many times. Each time, the generals did not do what Lincoln wanted. Lincoln read many books about war. He thought he was an expert. So, he gave the generals advice on how to fight the battles. They did not listen to him.

The First Draft

Toward the end of the war, not many men were volunteering for service. Lincoln started to use a **draft**. This meant that all men ages 20–45 could be forced to serve in the military. The men who were drafted could pay $300 to get out of the draft. Some men even hired someone else to take their places.

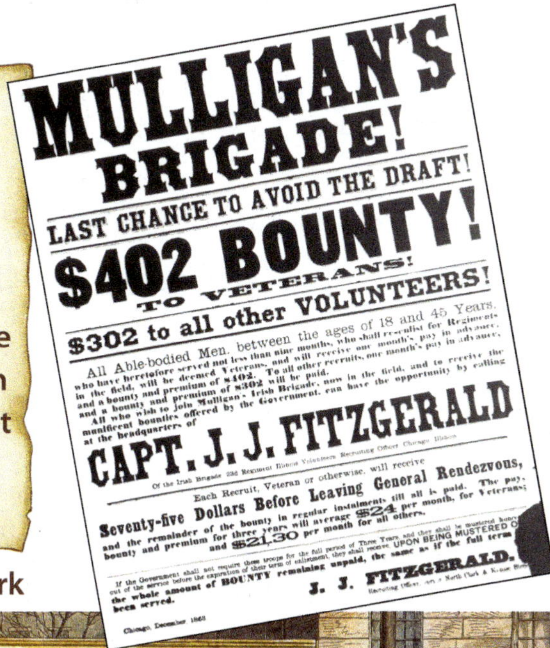

▼ Union recruiting station in New York

Lincoln wanted a general who could lead the North to victory. In 1864, Lincoln finally found the man for the job. He made General Ulysses S. Grant the new commander. Lincoln knew Grant was a fighter who would win many battles. Grant helped the North win the Civil War.

The Death of a President

The war ended on April 9, 1865. The southern general Robert E. Lee **surrendered** (suh-REN-duhrd) to the northern general Ulysses S. Grant. The two men met and signed an agreement to end the war.

John Wilkes Booth was a Southerner. He was upset that the South had lost the war. Booth wanted to be a hero to the South. He and some others created a plan to kill President Lincoln.

On April 14, 1865, Lincoln attended a play at Ford's Theatre in Washington, D.C. He was sitting in a special balcony seat with his wife and other guests.

John Wilkes Booth

Seeing Booth Before His Death

Booth was athletic and handsome. He came from an acting family and was very well known. Lincoln had even been to one of Booth's plays before.

This was where Booth shot President Lincoln in 1865.

Booth approached the balcony where Lincoln was sitting. Lincoln's guard had left his post. So, no one stopped Booth as he shot Lincoln in the head. Then, Booth jumped from the balcony onto the stage. As he escaped, Booth yelled, "*Sic semper tyrannis.*" This is Latin for "thus always to **tyrants**." He meant that all tyrants should be killed.

Lincoln died the next day. His vice president, Andrew Johnson, became the seventeenth president.

▲ Lincoln died in a house across the street from Ford's Theatre.

Don't Go!

A lot of people warned Lincoln not to go to the theater that night. Days before, Lincoln had dreamed that he was going to be killed. He did not listen to his advisors or his dreams.

Searching for Booth

John Wilkes Booth used a horse to escape from Ford's Theatre. He rode into Virginia. He thought that people in the South would be proud of what he had done. This was not the case.

This poster was printed to help catch Lincoln's killers.

Where Was Grant?

General Grant was supposed to attend the play with Lincoln that night. But, he cancelled at the last moment. Historians believe that Booth had planned to also kill Grant that night.

▲ The people who planned Lincoln's murder were hanged.

Most Southerners were upset over Lincoln's death. Lincoln would have wanted a peaceful **Reconstruction** (re-kuhn-STRUHK-shuhn). Now, they would have to deal with Congress instead of Lincoln. They were not sure what demands the congressmen would make.

Booth hid in a barn in Virginia. Federal troops found him, but he would not give up. The troops set the barn on fire. Then, troopers shot into the barn. Booth was killed. The people who had helped him plan the **assassination** were hanged.

Rebuilding a Nation

After the war, the southern states had to rejoin the Union. Then the Union needed to be rebuilt. The war had caused a lot of damage. These years were known as the Reconstruction.

Lincoln had planned to be easy on the South. He believed that leaders from each state in the South should give an oath of **loyalty** (LOY-uhl-tee) to the Union. He wanted to quickly accept the southern states back into the Union. Lincoln also wanted to ensure that ex-slaves were given equal rights.

▼ After the war, the Freedmen's Bureau helped blacks survive.

Helping the Freed Slaves

The Thirteenth Amendment freed the slaves forever. But, many ex-slaves still did not have land or homes. Some worked for very little pay on the same **plantations** (plan-TAY-shuhnz) they had worked on as slaves. The government set up the Freedmen's Bureau. This program provided food and education to the free blacks. It also helped poor whites in the South.

Unfortunately for the South, members of Congress made the rules. They did not want to treat the South nicely. President Andrew Johnson was not as strong or as popular as Lincoln. So, Johnson could not stand up to Congress.

If Lincoln had lived, the country would have had a better peace. He was a strong, intelligent, caring leader. He truly wanted what was best for the country and its people. The life and death of Lincoln changed American history in many ways.

President Andrew Johnson

▼ The country worked hard to reunite during the Reconstruction.

Glossary

assassination—when someone is killed for political reasons

ballots—papers used during an election to record votes

Border States—slave states that bordered free states

debates—formal talks between people about important issues

dedicate—set apart as special; give to a certain person or group of people

draft—an act stating one must join the military

electoral votes—the votes of people who elect the president as part of the Electoral College

emancipation—when someone is set free

honored—awarded; observed

loyalty—being true to a country or a person

majority—more than half

plantations—large farms that produced crops for money

popular vote—the votes of all the people in a democratic election

proclamation—an official government announcement

Reconstruction—the years after the Civil War when the country reformed

secede—to leave or break away from; states leaving the Union

slave auction—the public sale of slaves

surrendered—gave up and lost a battle or the war

turning point—the moment in a war where one side begins to win more of the battles; leads to the end of the war

tyrants—leaders who rule a country harshly; dictators